Thirty Days of Grief Prayers

Thirty Days of Grief Prayers

written by
Tom McGrath

illustrated by
R.W. Alley

ONE
CARING
PLACE
Abbey Press

Text © 2008 by Tom McGrath
Illustrations © 2008 by Saint Meinrad Archabbey
Published by One Caring Place
Abbey Press
St. Meinrad, Indiana 47577

Library of Congress Catalog Number
2008933815

ISBN 978-0-87029-417-4

Printed in the United States of America

Foreword

Grief comes to every life. If we engage in living, we will eventually experience loss, and loss means grief. The losses we experience can be big or small. Our personal losses may be something as minor as the loss of a familiar routine, or something as profound as the loss of someone we dearly love.

Every loss ought to be given its due. We do that by acknowledging whatever level of grief we are bearing, and giving grief the appropriate time, space, and attention to take its course. There is no set schedule for grieving; let the wisdom of your body guide you.

Prayer can help you through the many phases of grief-numbness, disbelief, anger, hurt, remorse, sadness, or even gratitude. The key is to pray from where you truly are—not where you suspect God thinks you should be. God wants the real you. Pray in the spirit of the Psalms, which means praying from the depths of your heart, letting God know what you're feeling. Don't hold back. Pray your way through grief and God will bring you, in due time, to a new wholeness and healing that incorporates your loss.

1.

Grief is not easy. Grieving can make you feel vulnerable and alone. So it's no wonder that our culture encourages people to quickly ignore their grief and "get on with life."

2.

But what could be more "true to life" than paying attention to what we're really feeling, and expressing those feelings honestly in prayer?

3.

It takes trust to grieve well, and courage to grieve fully. Grief may be uncomfortable, and even disturbing at times, but you don't have to enter into it alone.

4.

As you face the challenges of grief, know that God is close and caring. God meets us in our vulnerability and loneliness with strength and comfort and the reassurance that we are seen, understood, and loved.

5.

God longs to hear you tell about your many moods, your many questions, and your profound sense of loss.

6.

What follows are thirty days of prayers I jotted in my journal during my own season of grieving. I hope they help you find your own words of prayer and the encouragement to come before God—just as you are— each day.

7.

So often I fail to recognize those unbidden, unquiet feelings for what they are—grief over my recent loss. God, give me the grace to recognize grief when it comes, and to not turn away.

So often I fail to recognize those unbidden, unquiet feelings for what they are — grief over my recent loss. God, give me the grace to recognize grief when it comes, and not to turn away.

8.

Help me to trust in you, Lord, and to know that though my grief threatens to overwhelm me, there's nothing that you and I together cannot handle. Walk with me, Lord.

9.

Grief sometimes feels as though I'm an alien in a foreign land. I don't know the language or the customs. I feel cut off from everyone else. God, you seek out those who are lost. I pray that you will find me in this unfamiliar place.

10.

There are days when my life seems ruled by fear, and days when I walk in faith. As one grows, the other diminishes. Help me to choose faith, Lord, especially when fear creeps in.

11.

Today I feel weak, Lord. I know if I push away my weakness, I push you away as well. If I let myself feel my weakness, you are near with your strength and your comfort. Help me to trust.

12.

Nighttime is the hardest, Lord. Just before I drift off to sleep all the deep feelings I covered over during the day come to the surface. Help me, then, Lord, even when I forget to ask your help.

13.

Help me to have patience with those who want me to feel different than I'm feeling, the ones who want to hurry my grieving along. Let me take their words as a sign of their loving concern.

14.

I realize that I've been isolating myself lately—avoiding people and situations, not out of self-care, but out of fear. I feel I have no courage right now, God. Let me borrow yours to do the next right thing I need to do.

15.

Today I just want to take a break from grieving, Lord. I want to live today without the heaviness of heart that accompanies me so often. God, help me to know it is okay to lay down my grief for a time.

16.

God, give me the wisdom to know when I ought to take time alone, and when it's better to get back into the swing of life again. I find myself confused, and I ask your gentle guidance on my way.

17.

Today I felt joy for the first time in a while when I bit into and really tasted a fresh, ripe peach. Help me, God, to know the joy of simple, healthy pleasures. I know they're all around me if I have the eyes to see them.

18.

Help me, Lord, not to fight off uncomfortable feelings of grief, but to embrace them. Help me to know that despite my fear, with your help they won't overwhelm me.

19.

God, today I have no words to pray. My tears will have to be my prayer. They are plentiful.

20.

I watched a venerable old tree in our neighborhood being cut down today. I've enjoyed that tree through many seasons—its shade in summer, its stark, snow-covered limbs in winter, and the amazing transformations that took place each spring and fall. I'm glad I know how to grieve.

21.

God, today I'm on the verge of despair. Help me to be mindful of all the gifts you've given, even the ones I'm mourning the loss of today. Help me to hang on to gratitude as the appropriate antidote to despair and fear.

22.

Caring for myself usually falls low on my list of things to do. Somehow I got the message that self-care equals selfish. You have given me my life. Help me to care for it, and myself, as you would want.

23.

At the zoo with my family today I was flooded by memories of my own childhood outings with family members who have since passed away. God, I offer you the whole package of my day—the joy, the grief, the sadness, the gratitude. It's all yours.

24.

Today I want solid answers, Lord, but you seem silent. Rather than certainty, you invite me into the mystery of your love. Give me the courage to accept what you offer.

25.

Dear God, I have no words to pray today. I know that others who love me are praying for me. I will let their prayers carry me through today.

26.

Soften my heart, O God. I am tempted to shield my heart with armor so that I won't hurt anymore. You know that love can hurt, but you invite us to love anyway. Don't let me grow hard-hearted.

27.

Through prayer I realize these days of grieving are a mosaic, Lord. Each day, different from the rest, is put in place bearing its own shape, tone, and texture. Help me to see in the larger picture that you are always with me, Lord.

28.

Sometimes I'm surprised by grief when it shows up as a flash of impatience or a vacant disinterest in things that used to bring me joy. It's helpful to realize that this is grief and it, too, shall pass.

29.

Thank you, God, for the company of those who have learned how to grieve. Their hearts are wide enough to make room for the grief of others. They are a blessing.

30.

God, give me patience with
myself and with this slow
process of grieving. Give me the
grace to treat myself with care,
no matter how long it takes.

31.

God, help me to stay in the present moment. I'm so tempted to look achingly at the past, or anxiously toward the future. Teach me to live serenely in the now.

DONATION
BOX

32.

Today I went to church and found myself silent through the whole service. I didn't sing. I voiced no prayers. I sat empty, grateful for the community who sang and prayed while I could not.

33.

God, it's the middle of the night. I lie awake feeling sadness and fear. I remember your promise to be with me in trying times. Are you here?

34.

Help me, God, to accept my own complexity. I can be sorrowful and still know joy. I can be angry at you and still long for your closeness. Thank you for making room for all of me, however I show up.

35.

Lord, thank you for this wonderful day in which I feel alive and joyful once again. Thank you for the reminder that life continues and life's gifts await me.

36.

God, help me to trust in the ultimate goodness of life. Fill my heart with your love so that I may have a foretaste of life everlasting united with you and all my loved ones. Amen.

37.

Grief is an invitation to care for your soul. Prayer is a way of accepting God's offer to walk that path alongside you.

38.

God waits patiently for you, and prayer is the key that will open the door. Receive the gift of praying through your grief.

Tom McGrath is vice president of New Product Development for Loyola Press and the author of *Raising Faith-Filled Kids* (2000, Loyola Press). He lives in Chicago with his wife Kathleen.

Illustrator for the Abbey Press Elf-help Books, **R.W. Alley**, also illustrates and writes children's books, including *Making a Boring Day Better—A Kid's Guide to Battling the Blahs*, a recent Elf-help Book for Kids. See a wide variety of his works at: www.rwalley.com.

The Story of the Abbey Press Elves

The engaging figures that populate the Abbey Press "elf-help" line of publications and products first appeared in 1987 on the pages of a small self-help book called *Be-good-to-yourself Therapy*. Shaped by the publishing staff's vision and defined in R.W. Alley's inventive illustrations, they lived out the author's gentle, self-nurturing advice with charm, poignancy, and humor.

Reader response was so enthusiastic that more Elf-help Books were soon under way, a still-growing series that has inspired a line of related gift products.

The especially endearing character featured in the early books—sporting a cap with a mood-changing candle in its peak—has since been joined by a spirited female elf with flowers in her hair.

These two exuberant, sensitive, resourceful, kindhearted, lovable sprites, along with their lively elfin community, reveal what's truly important as they offer messages of joy and wonder, playfulness and co-creation, wholeness and serenity, the miracle of life and the mystery of God's love.

With wisdom and whimsy, these little creatures with long noses demonstrate the elf-help way to a rich and fulfilling life.

Elf-help Books

...adding "a little character" and a lot
of help to self-help reading!

Book price is $4.95 unless otherwise noted.
Available at your favorite gift shop or bookstore—
or directly from One Caring Place, Abbey Press
Publications, St. Meinrad, IN 47577.
Or call 1-800-325-2511.
www.carenotes.com